ABOUT POTATO
A BRIEF OVERVIEW

I FIRST STARTED RIDING horses around the age of 10 at a local riding stable, B Bar M Ranch, near my home in Troy, Michigan. There were close to 100 horses at the B-M and there was always something to do. In exchange for helping with the ranch chores, we boys were allowed to ride the horses. Many of my close friends had their own horses, but I only had a horse to ride at the B-M. The first Arabian horse I ever saw was a great mare owned by a friend and he let me ride her in gymkhana classes. This was in Michigan in the mid-50s, and there were not many Arabian horses around at that time. She was an awesome mare who was easy to ride, and we won events like pole bending and pick-up races.

My next opportunity to really get back to having a horse was in 1972 when I rented an apartment from ten-time Tevis buckle recipient and Haggin Cup winner Paige Harper. Paige had a wonderful place called Ranch Apartments with 10 two-bedroom rentals and a ten-stall barn. Rent was $140 a month and $25 more if you had a horse. Paige did the daily care of the horses including feed and stall cleaning. It was perfect for me. When I saw the Tevis logo on his truck rear window and his Tevis buckle, I was hooked. Paige helped me buy my first endurance horse — an Appaloosa named Grazeagle Bandit. My first endurance ride was Tevis 1973, riding Grazeagle Bandit. My next horse was Eden's Cailana AHR # 46450. I bought her on a package deal — the mare and a 9N Ford tractor. As of now (2015), of the 31 times I started Tevis, I have finished 22 times, finishing Top Ten nine times and winning the Tevis Cup three times. In the 43 years I have been involved in Tevis, I have helped many riders from all over the world ride and complete. I have also competed in endurance rides in many different countries worldwide, sometimes on my own horse. All of my three children have earned Tevis Buckles

POLE#1

MENTORS
AND ICONS
PAIGE AND WENDELL

P AIGE HARPER IS the man who introduced me to Tevis. Paige, a two-time Haggin Cup winner (the award presented to the horse judged to be in best condition among the first ten to finish), earned his 1000 mile buckle in 1977 and passed away early 1978. After Paige passed away, Dru Barner (the first woman to win the Tevis Cup and Wendell Robie's assistant) and I helped build a monument to Paige along the trail from the Highway 49 trail crossing, leading to what at that time was a veterinary checkpoint at a place near Cool, California called Pointed Rocks. There is a small spring along that trail, and Paige and I would quite often clean it up and keep it clear for horses to get a drink of water.

Paige, who rode Tevis the first time in 1958, owned a terrific complex called Ranch Apartments located in Sacramento near the California State Horsemen's Association (CSHA) stable facility. It originally was what would be called a "ranchette" today. He had his ranch house there and built a ten unit apartment complex on the edge of the property. Each unit had two bedrooms and a carport. The barn had ten stalls, each with an outside paddock. The apartment rent when I moved there in 1972 was $140/month plus $25 more if you had a horse. That included feed and care for the horse. Paige took care of cleaning and feeding daily, so it was a great place to live. He had a nice swimming pool and riding arena as well as a good trail system around Haggin Oaks Golf Course that also connected to the CSHA stables. It was a perfect place to get in a nice ride from home without having to trailer. When I spotted the Tevis buckle on Paige, and the picture of a buckle on his pick-up rear window, I was hooked. In 1972 Paige helped me purchase my first endurance horse from a man named Ratzy Manaro — an Appaloosa named Grazeagle aBandit. *(See fig. 1)*

Paige introduced me to Wendell Robie and Dru Barner, and before long I was a member of the Board of Directors for the Western States Trails Foundation, an organization founded by Wendell Robie. Wendell was president of a business in Auburn, Central California Federal Savings and Loan, and he often bragged that his was the only S&L in the nation that did not owe the Federal Government a single dime. Once a year a few of us would ride with Wendell to Emigrant Pass (8750') above Squaw Valley to put up the American flag at the Watson Monument. Another annual trip that Dru would ask Paige and me to do was to check if the large tank at Horsemen's Park was filling up with water okay. Horsemen's Park was a favorite spot just below White Oaks Flat on the Tevis Trail where vet checks were held after the Echo Hills vet check was closed.

Wendell and Dru, along with Paige, quickly became some of my favorite people. One remark I often recall, when asked if he would ride the first part of the trail

Fig 1: Photo: Wendell had this one horse trailer built in 1947, I bought it for $100 bucks 1977

Photo Credit: Dominique Cognee

out of Squaw to help mark trail Paige would say, "I only need to ride that section once a year." Dru was a wonderful woman who everybody adored. It didn't take long to realize how powerful a man Wendell was. I will never forget the day he asked me to escort California Governor Ronald Reagan on the Tevis. Reagan said, "By golly, if I can show the nation that I can ride 100 miles in one day on a horse, I can certainly show the nation how I can run this country as president."

Wendell would often address me as Robert at formal meetings, so his letter to Governor Reagan said, "Robert Richardson will be your escort on the ride." The Governor asked who Robert Richardson was, and the man presenting the letter explained that it was me. Governor Reagan said, "Potato's first name is Robert?" The Governor knew of me from riding out of CSHA, but only as Potato. Governor Reagan was a horseman, but he never did ride Tevis. However, he was quoted as certainly showing a strong interest in wanting to do so.

Wendell had connections all over the world and was a very prominent and industrious businessman. He knew how to get things done and done quickly. He would ask me to make a list of candidates to put on the WSTF Board, because there would be a few openings each year. I once asked him why a certain person was on the board because I had never heard of him. Wendell said that he was in charge of the US Forest Service and we needed him at times (he was also related to a past California governor). Wendell had well placed connections worldwide, and he used them to his advantage — often to help with the Tevis Trail.

Paige and I would often trailer to Robie Point in Auburn and ride out to the river and back or we'd trailer to Michigan Bluff and ride the canyons. Those years the Foresthill vet stop was downtown in a vacant lot at the corner of California Street and Foresthill Road. The current location of the vet stop in Foresthill used to be a lumber mill where we rode up Bath Road to Foresthill Road and then into town for the vet check (a number of riders would get ice cream at the drive-in along the way). After clearing the vet check, we traveled out of town along the road past the fire station, then turned left on a trail to Todd Valley.

The next one-hour vet check was at a great place called Echo Hills Ranch. The last year the ride went through Echo Hills Ranch was 1975. That's the year I earned my first Tevis buckle, riding a horse I borrowed named Maariner. We had a total riding time of 20 hours and 2 minutes, finishing in 86th place out of 96 finishers; 163 riders started so the ride had a 60% completion.

As a matter of fact, the last year we had the vet check at Echo Hills Ranch, which was in 1975. The Wednesday before the ride Wendell called on me to take a tree off the trail that had fallen down between the river crossing at Poverty Bar and Echo Hills Ranch. Shirley Gregory and I saddled up that evening and I carried a small chain saw up that grade to remove the tree. The next day Dru and Wendell were so appreciative that Dru told me that from then on I would be wearing number 1 on the ride. Those days, there were quite a few riders who had the same number every year. The exception was Doc Barsaleau DVM who often had the habit of asking for the number that was his age that year. The system that's in place now makes perfect sense, and I like it. Of course, like most things in life, it's subject to change.

POLE #2

GETTING TO THE STARTING LINE— LITERALLY

L ET ME START by saying that many people think getting to the starting line is the hardest part of riding Tevis — the toughest 100 mile endurance ride in the world. And it may be, if you interpret that phrase as incorporating all the miles, sweat, money, energy and fortitude it takes to build up the stamina and spirit to qualify yourself and your mount for this world class 100-mile tough, tough ride.

But let me tell you about literally getting through the pre-ride vet check and on to the starting line.

Personally, in all the 43 years I've been around the Tevis, I have never had a difficult time getting to the starting line. Sure, a couple of times I was challenged at vetting in my horse, but I don't ever recall any overwhelming challenge in getting to the starting line.

However, the worst time before the actual ride was in 1979 when the ride started in Squaw Valley. Volunteers were helping me, and a gal from back east who I met at the Old Dominion Ride came out to crew for me and to experience Tevis. She unloaded my mare, Eden's Cailana, from my two-horse ramp trailer without untying her. When the mare got to the end of the lead rope she was halfway out and it spooked her. She stepped sideways and her rear leg slipped off the ramp, causing serious cuts inside the leg. There must have been five or six vets to the rescue; the wound was very bad. Finally, Cailana was bandaged and I loaded her back into the trailer to take her home. I will never forget how she was trembling and upset. I walked into the trailer and just put my hand on her rump and she calmed right down. Eden's Cailana is the foundation mare of nearly all my horses; she was truly a wonderful animal in so many ways.

So in 1979 I was out of a mount to ride. This was a big disappointment to many (including me!) because the year before I was the first one across the finish line, which in those years was at Robie Point — the crest of the canyon that leads to Auburn. However, I ended up in second place because back then the riders started in groups of 10, two minutes apart. Kathie Perry had an 8-minute advantage because she started 4 groups behind me, so when she crossed the finish line three minutes behind me, she had won the Tevis Cup by five minutes.

Before the mare was injured at Tevis in 1979, all eyes (and bets) had been on Eden's Cailana — we had been winning 50-mile rides earlier that year and were placing well on every ride. After Cailana was injured so badly, another rider offered me her horse who had already been checked in and was ready to go. The rider told me she really was scared to ride but was actually there just to prove her horse could do it. Her ranch was breeding a certain line of Arabian horses and to finish Tevis on them would be a very big plus for that particular type of Arabian horse. She really was afraid of the challenge of Tevis and did not want to ride. So at the last minute, in spite of the mishap to my mount, I still had a horse to ride. I was fortunate to have someone capable of taking care of Cailana while I continued on to the ride. But little did I know that this new horse was not in shape to go 100 miles and had never been on any hills higher than a berm alongside a ditch. Boyd Zontelli won that year in 11 hours and 33 minutes — nearly a half hour ahead of second place rider Lori Stewart. I crossed the finish line at Robie Point at 4:40 a.m. in 122nd place after riding for 19 hours and 35 minutes. That was a lot longer than the year before when I finished in 12 hours and 22 minutes! That year 162 riders finished out of 227 starters, making it 71% completion rate.

Another year when I had a challenge getting started was in 1984. I had five horses ready to start Tevis, and five days before the ride as I was shopping in Auburn, I looked across the horizon and saw horrible clouds of smoke rising up from the direction of my ranch. Following a strong gut feeling, I rushed home — a 20 minute drive — and just as I entered my driveway I saw county animal control officers herding my horses from the main barn down the driveway to a safe place away from the burning buildings. As a result of that 210-acre fire that roared through my property, I lost one barn and my water well house, and the acreage sustained lots of other damage. Thank goodness the firemen saved my house and many of the other structures. However, three of the five horses I had ready for Tevis were injured in that chaos and were unable to start.

At that time I had four riders from France at my ranch — Stephane Chazel, Denis and Marie Letartre, and Christophe Pelissier — all anxious to ride Tevis on my horses. Christophe, now a veterinarian, and Stephane were both young boys (age 16) and were at my ranch for the summer along with a gal, who I best recall was from Switzerland. Denis, Stephane and Christophe were very involved in the endurance world and still are to this day. Denis Letartre is very immersed in the FEI world in France and Stephane raises super endurance Arabs in France. His parents are very involved in the Florac 160 km ride in France that many call the French Tevis Cup. Christophe is the team vet for the French national endurance team and Marie Letartre (now Marie Deroubaix-Leprince) owns a B&B in France.

Anyway, that year, because of help from great friends, I was able to secure replacement mounts and the five of us started Tevis 1984. Only Christophe, who ended up riding an Appaloosa that I borrowed, did not finish.

I will never forget that summer. One evening four of us decided to take a moonlight ride and the four of us (Christophe, Stephane, the Swiss girl and I) rode out to a small lake nearby and took the horses in the water for a swim. On the way home, riding along a roadway on my horse Hassan, Christophe was along beside me when Hassan quickly snapped out a warning to Christophe to stay away. The next thing I knew Christophe was jumping up and down on the roadway, holding his crotch and yelling, "He bit me! He bit me!" I thought my horse just challenged his mount, but that was not the case. It was dark and difficult to see all the commotion, but Christophe was certainly in overwhelming pain. Upon a brief (literally) examination the next morning Christophe was given the nickname "Blue Balls" and I think it sticks with his close friends still to this day.

Another big challenge to starting Tevis was in 1997 when National Geographic Television series asked me to assist them in producing a television special on the Tevis. The initial plan was for Boyd Matson, the on-air personality of the 30-minute television program, to ride the event and they would film it. I explained that the completion ratio for well-experienced riders was about 50%, and that the chances he would have with film crews and all the personnel and paraphernalia would be probably zero. We finally agreed that I would assist them with riding certain parts of the trail. That would give them all they needed for good coverage. At the time I had riders at my ranch from Brazil, Hungary, France and the UK. Needless to say it was a bit busy.

When the National Geographic crew arrived one day early to fit cameras on the horses' halters, the fun began. Boyd and I actually started the ride that year. However, the plan was to ride to Robinson Flat (about 36 miles) then trailer the horse and rider to Foresthill and take up the trail from that location on to Auburn — avoiding the canyons. That Tevis ride turned out to be an experience that deserves a whole book by itself. While we made it to the starting line, we never intended to do the whole ride and we certainly didn't. Needless to say, the short recording of that particular National Geographic program is one of my favorite videos to this day. On the tenth anniversary of the National Geo program, Boyd was asked which episode from the past ten years was his most memorable. He responded with, "Riding the Tevis 100 Mile One Day Ride with Potato Richardson."

The only other time I had difficulty starting was in 2007 when my stallion SMR Garcon, who took me to a 3rd place finish in 2006, was a bit off at the vetting in at Robie Park. In 2005 he was also a bit off at the Tevis veterinary check-in, so I saddled him and had a serious talk with him while I rode a mile or so. When I returned to the check-in he was sound and passed the vetting criteria without a problem. That caused quite a stir, to say the least, with the vets who were amazed that he passed. So in 2007 a new rule was incorporated that once you entered the vetting area, you were not allowed to leave without a "pass" or "no pass" vet check card. Interesting that there were several times during that 2006 ride on SMR Garcon when the vets drew blood to verify that he was "clean." There are several new rules instigated over the years I call "Potato Rules" (I will cover a few more later in this book). Anyway, because I was not allowed in 2007 to take Garcon out and talk to him during a warm-up (as I had the previous year), I was a bit upset. So I had a friend go to my ranch and get SMR Zoltaan, a gelding by Garcon who I had bred and raised. However, we only had a few miles on him which included a 50-miler when Drew Beuchley rode him a month earlier.

So I started the 2007 Tevis journey on Zoltaan and he was a bit of a handful. The vets, while vetting him in at the pre-ride check, could not get his pulse below 94 — yet all his other indications were very good, so it was obvious that his high heart rate was due to the fact that he was anxious. We even brought his sire Garcon over to try and help calm him down, but nothing helped. Thankfully, the vets in their good judgment could see Zoltaan's anxiety and passed him to start the ride. I might add that riding Zoltaan in 2007 I was 4th into Red Star Ridge and the three riders ahead of me did not finish. And I was 8th into Robinson Flat. When I was ready to leave Robinson Flat they were doing a Cardiac Recovery Index which consists of hand trotting the horse out a ways and back ("CRI," an indication of fitness to continue) on the top ten horses ready to leave. Zoltaan's pulse was 56 before the CRI. He was 94 after the CRI and normally an 8-beat increase is grounds for a pull. Going from 56 to 94 was a bit over the limit — like 28 points over the limit — but once again the vet could see that he was excited. Zoltaan kept looking around and whinnying while all his other signs were excellent. We were allowed to continue. When we finished the Tevis in 38th place, he had less than 200 miles under saddle. The next Tevis for Zoltaan, in 2009, he placed 7th. Not bad for a "green" gray.

So contrary to that often-heard statement, I have not had much trouble starting Tevis.

Incidentally, another "Potato Rule" was established in 2003. That was the year that starting in holding pens was instigated, rather than in the previous years when riders were sectioned off along the road from Robie Park to the start which is about a mile out. I recall Western

States Trail Foundation (WSTF) President Bill Pieper at the pre-ride meeting Friday night in 2002 instructing the riders as follows: "If you want to ride with Potato go the third flag which is at the starting line. If you're not interested in going that speed, stop at the second flag, and if you are just concerned about finishing, stop at the first flag." He was adamant in directing the riders to stay on the side of the dirt road that led to the starting line to let other riders pass by to the flags farther up. That year there were a lot of riders at the second flag and it was rather difficult to pass by to get to the first flag. It was such a ruckus that the next year the holding pen system was incorporated. Now the horses are released from a holding pen #1 and after they have left, the holding pen #2 is released and so on. It is a controlled start for the first mile to the actual starting point. Why they don't just start from the exit of pen #1 is a mystery to me. It is still essentially a controlled start when they open the gate to let the riders out of pen #1 followed by pen #2 and so on. So in the 31 times I have ridden Tevis, only a few times have I had a challenge starting and I did it anyway. This year 2015 was not even a slight problem as SMR Filouette was in tip-top shape.

POLE #3

CONQUERING COUGAR ROCK
LEFT TURN OR RIGHT TURN?

W HEN THE RIDE started this year Gabriella Valsecchi, #204, was riding my mare SMR Fifi d'Or, who won the Tevis Cup in 2005. I was riding SMR Filouette, #13, and we were off and setting a nice pace. Filouette is just like her dam Fille de Cailana — who took me across the finish line to win the Tevis Cup in 1998. She's also like her granddam Eden's Cailana who gave me such wonderful rides in the 1970's. Filouette is an absolute charm to ride. She is easy to control, yet seems to always have energy in reserve to give that extra speed if needed. I think of it as the "Seabiscuit surge" and once you experience it you will never forget it. I think in my 40-plus years of riding I have only experienced it a handful of times and it is absolutely fantastic.

In all the many years I've traveled that historic trail, 31 to be exact, each year the ride from the start (no matter which starting location — Squaw Valley in the early years and now Robie Park) has always been absolutely beautiful, climbing magnificent Emigrant Pass, the colors of the flowers, the views of the mountains and valleys as well as the wildlife and even the few bent trees made so by the weight of the heavy snow that often falls on these high Sierra Nevada mountains. Sometimes

Fig 2: Photo: Gore/Baylor Photography

there's a remaining snowdrift still waiting to add to the yearning reservoirs below for thirsty humans. Yes, this first section is indeed breathtakingly beautiful.

I have to state here that in the whole 100 miles of the ride this year 2015, I firmly believe I never rode faster than a trot for more than a total of 50 feet. Yet, somehow, invariably Gabriella and I rode alone for most of the time along the way to Red Star with no one in front of us or even close behind us. We saw no riders until we stopped at Hodgsons Cabin (20 miles from the start) and they came in just a minute behind us. Then after we passed Hodgson's Cabin by about a mile, as best I recall rider #51 was the first one to pass us then #178. We pretty much were alone except for a couple of riders all the way to Red Star Ridge vet check.

As usual, the first riders into a vet check, or in this case Cougar Rock, are often greeted by a bit of confusion. The year 2015 was no exception. As we approached Cougar Rock, a person was standing out in front who seemed to be guiding riders to the bypass so they did not have to climb the "Rock," and before I knew it — I was close behind #178 — Gabriella and I were on the Cougar Rock bypass trail. As soon as I realized that, I reined to the left over the bushes and Gabriella and I were the first two to climb Cougar Rock. Because of that minor detour, when we returned to the trail after the Rock we had two more riders in front of us. From that point on there were a number of riders close behind us, but I have no idea how many as I don't look back often and do not have eyes in the back of my head.

POLE #4

ARRIVING AT RED STAR, READY TO GO— AND THEN ON TO ROBINSON FLAT WITH RIDERS HOT ON OUR TAILS

G ABRIELLA AND I rode into the Red Star vet check just moments ahead of several riders and as usual, Fifi was ready to go — she has incredible recovery and I was just a few minutes behind her on Filouette. Shannon Yewell Weil took pulses of Filouette and Fifi d'Or and here's her comment: "Taking pulses at the Red Star Ridge vet check is one of my favorite things to do during the Tevis Cup Ride 100-mile challenge. To me, it's a chance to listen to a symphony of the horses' heart music. I hear strings, horns, winds and big base drums all in the form of ka-booms and ka-plunks while horses are resting to meet the 60 beats per minute criteria. When Potato Richardson's two chestnut mares arrived at Red Star in 2015, I offered to take their pulses. First SMR Fifi D'Or, ridden by Gabriella Valsecchi. I listened for a minute and was struck by what I heard. Then I moved over to Potato's mount, the lovely SMR Filouette. Again I was stunned by what I heard. These two mares had a sound of their own. After 28 miles on the trail, and in the midst of chaotic activity, both of these mares' heartbeats were smooth and succinct. It sounded like I was listening to fine precision Swiss watches. Low, smooth and very steady, unencumbered by the challenge of the day unlike any other heartbeat I had heard all morning. The quality of these two mares is reflected on the breeding program that Potato has continued over the past thirty years, stemming from his foundation mare, Eden's Cailana."

I was amazed at how nice and smooth Filouette's heart rate was. There were four of us riders who left Red Star Ridge together — #178 and #10 Karen Donley along with Gabriella and me. However, there were over 20 riders just minutes behind us, but once more because I don't have eyes in the back of my head I never saw them again. Perhaps another reason I never saw them again was because halfway between Red Star Ridge vet check and Robinson Flat a well-known volunteer, Robert Sydnor, was on duty with water troughs for the riders. Most riders are prone to try to get their horses to stop and drink at every opportunity. My horses are trained to let me know if they want water. When they want water they are very clear about it. I have been using a special water at the ranch for years called "Living Water," also known as Revitalized Water. It is definitely very healthy and my horses love it. As a matter of fact, I haul it with me on rides and when I run out my horse complains a little.

One year when I took one of my horses on her first Tevis, it was practically the first time she had to drink at a public trough. I will never forget that at Pieper Junction (at that time it was called Chicken Hawk) she looked at the water and didn't drink, went to the next tub again and didn't drink, and so on to the third and the last tub. She sniffed the water, looked around for another place to drink, and when she didn't see any, she drank from that last tub. I keep a close eye on my horses, always assessing how much they eat and drink so I know if something is different. They definitely prefer my Living Water.

Moving on, Gabriella and I came into Robinson Flat just 3 minutes behind #178 and lots of riders hot on our tail not too far back. One of the most amazing things happened at Robinson Flat and it was the first time in the 40-plus years I have been involved with Tevis. A cloud storm burst open overhead with a pretty hard downpour of rain. It was brief, but it was enough to get the crews scurrying to keep things dry. It didn't last long and I welcomed it.

As luck would have it, Fifi d'Or slipped on the shale rocky trail in Squaw Valley and that slip revealed itself at Robinson Flat as a problem. And Gabriella was pulled from the ride. However, we both remarked as we rode those first 20 miles of the ride that the scenery was so fantastic — with the variation of beautiful flowers and green grass as well as the views — that it was worth the whole effort just to see that beauty. So in spite of Gabriella not continuing on, she had a great time.

POLE #5

NEAR-TRAGEDY ALONG PUCKER POINT TRAIL; RESPITE AT LAST CHANCE

M EANWHILE, AS I was about to leave Robinson Flat, I discovered there was only one rider
ahead of me and that was #178. You never really know
for sure unless you do some scouting around for who
is ahead of you, ready to leave, until you get to the out
timer because the arrival time is not the same time as
when your hold starts. The one-hour mandatory time
starts when your horse's pulse reaches a certain level,
usually 60 beats per minute. So if a rider races into the
vet stop at a gallop, that horse will most likely take longer to recover to a heart rate of 60 beats per minute.
That is one reason I normally remove the saddle as soon
as possible when I enter a vet check, as it lets the horse
relax quicker and it is easier to cool them down. Rider
#178's out time was one minute before mine, so she had
a one-minute lead on me. We chatted a bit and I discovered she was from the UK but I didn't catch her name
as the excitement at the out timers is always a bit hectic.

Since #178 only had a minute head start on me, it
was no problem to catch up to her. The trail out of Robinson Flat is a gravel road for what seems like 50 miles,
so we had plenty of time to ride together and chat a bit.
I was not aware that she was riding the horse that won

the Tevis Cup the year before, and I had no idea that she apparently was chosen to ride the Tevis because she was the choice of a very organized effort to find the best rider possible to win the 60th running of the Tevis on the horse that won in 2014. I did ask her why she didn't climb over Cougar Rock and she said Hillary Bachman the owner of the horse told her not to. I replied in my naive nature, "Well, if I was leasing a horse to ride Tevis and was told not to go over Cougar, I would find a different horse to ride." Little did I know she was, in reality, a fully-sponsored rider who had definite instructions on how to win.

Anyway, we finally approached the point where the trail left the gravel road. There were water troughs at that point where several riders caught up to us. I never got their numbers but I recall they were low numbers. The rider numbering system is such that the top ten riders the year before are given the same number as their finish, so the winning rider the year before would be #1 this year, and so on for the first ten. Then numbers 11 to 20 are normally reserved for previous Tevis Cup winners, so that is why I was #13 this year. In addition, numbers starting in the 20's are reserved for foreign riders. They all stopped for water and Filouette took a quick drink; she probably didn't like the water much but she needed a sip and we left ahead of them all. The trail from there on was a dusty dirt downhill jeep road and it wasn't long before those riders who I left at the water tubs flew past me at a very fast pace. I was happy about that because they raised a lot of dust and it was several miles of that dirt road. The trail then broke out on another gravel road that leads to Last Chance and about a quarter mile down was another stop with water troughs and refreshments for the riders. When I arrived, those riders who had passed me were watering their horses and Filouette took a few quick drinks. I grabbed a couple slices of watermelon from the great volunteers who were very helpful. I then left that stop ahead of the other riders who had passed me earlier.

I continued on to Pucker Point trail. It should be called Pucker POINTS trail as there are many places that could be fatal if you were to fall off the edge. Anyway, it was a bit disconcerting that there were no yellow ribbons marking the trail. Because there were lots of switchbacks, it gave me a good chance to see if there were any riders behind me. I saw absolutely none. I could have sworn I did not see any other way to go, and about that time I approached a tree across the trail. It wasn't a problem to go around it, but that added to the concern of lack of yellow ribbons. No riders catching up to me was strange. Was I on the wrong trail I asked myself.

Anyway, I continued on and next thing I know, I find a large tree across the trail that was definitely too high to jump over and too low to go under. I tried to climb up the bank, but it was too steep. Filouette tried, but she couldn't go up and the down side was definitely not a good way to go. So I climbed up the hill on my hands and feet and thankfully I had long reins so I could urge Filouette up the steep bank. Without me on her back she was able to maneuver this vertical obstacle. As I scurried around the up-rooted trunk, I slipped and fell down the bank for about 25 feet, and I actually envisioned my demise as I tumbled down. Fortunately I landed on the trail and didn't continue off the other side of the canyon, which could have been fatal. However, my back was in pain, my arm bloody and I was so out of breath I couldn't mount my horse who came down when I tugged on the reins — otherwise she was just standing part-way up the bank looking at me. I led her for quite a while on foot until I got my breath back, and then I rode on into the Last Chance vet check. The climb up and around that big tree in my mind was a bigger challenge than Cougar Rock. *(See fig. 3)*

Doug Van Howd, the world famous sculpture artist, and others are the organizers of that vet check and it's always a pleasure to be there — they have super volunteers and lots of goodies. The Last Chance vet check is important because it's the starting point to the biggest canyon on the ride. The vets look closely at the horses here; what's next on the trail shouldn't be ridden on less than a strong horse. This vet check is also staffed by very experienced people who go to every possible effort to help. I informed the people at the stop about the trees on the trail and they were anxious to resolve that problem. The medical personnel at the stop put a bandage on my bloody arm and I vetted my mare through. As I was leaving, I saw riders coming in.

TEVIS 2015

POTATO RICHARDSON #13- FIRST TO THE HALFWAY MARK AT LAST CHANCE.

TIME: 11:48 A.M.

Fig 3: Photo credit: Nancy Van Houd

POLE #6

CHALLENGING THE CANYONS; ENDLESS SWITCHBACKS TO DEVIL'S THUMB; LIVELY DEADWOOD

S O FROM THAT point I entered the first big canyon, where the rebuilt Swinging Bridge resides at the bottom. As I have every year, I rode down into the river to give my mount a drink. But this year Chuck Gabri and his crew were there assisting riders. I crossed the river and climbed up the other side without going up and over the bridge. I thought I heard another rider, who turned out to be rider #4, as I started up the canyon but I wasn't sure. There are 43 switchbacks climbing out of that canyon and Filouette was anxious to get to the top at Devil's Thumb. We rode alone and there were plenty of possibilities to see any riders behind us.

Just as we got near the top of the canyon to Devil's Thumb, I heard another rider and so did Filouette. It's a hot and hard climb, but she quickened her pace just like her grand-dam Cailana did many years ago. When we got to the top at Devil's Thumb, there were plenty of volunteers there with water for the horses and drinks for me. I never did see the rider behind me at that short stop. We lingered for a few minutes then continued on, still without any other riders in sight. The next stop is a vet stop about a mile from Devil's Thumb called Deadwood. I arrived there alone and vetted through without a problem. Most of the vet controls are what are called a "gate and go" which means once your horse meets a certain pulse rate, normally 60 beats per minute, you have the vet examine the horse for soundness and fitness to go on, and you leave. It's called a trot out after the vet checks the horse for metabolics and any apparent abrasions, etc. As I was about to leave, I did see rider #4 ride in. After the Deadwood vet check there's another canyon that takes the rider up to an old mining town called Michigan Bluff.

Years ago there was a one-hour vet check in Michigan Bluff. It was always a very popular stop and certainly much easier to maneuver than Robinson Flat is today, so it's a shame that Michigan Bluff is not used anymore for a vet stop.

When Michigan Bluff was a mandatory one-hour vet stop, the number of riders with crew people helping them made it very difficult to safely handle the crowd. So now it's just a place for the riders to give their horse a drink of water. A few people still go there to assist their riders. There is a nice little stream about a mile before the arrival at Michigan Bluff and Filouette drank all she needed. The climb up the canyon is probably one of the hottest parts of the ride, and there is even a place near there called Bake Oven — appropriately named. So when we arrived in Michigan Bluff we didn't spend much time there as the next vet check, Pieper Junction (formerly called Chicken Hawk), is just a few miles away.

POLE #7

SPAGHETTI ROADS
AT
PIEPER JUNCTION

P IEPER JUNCTION WAS in a new location from the year before, and Filouette was a bit concerned when we passed the spot where it was previously located — she has incredible memory. Filouette has been ridden on Tevis every year for the last seven years, so she knows the trail very well. Turns out the new location has a lot more room and is very accommodating to the needs of a good vet check. The big difference to me was the trail out of that vet check was not the straight path of the prior year, but more like intersection of the freeways in downtown El Paso, Texas. The El Paso intersection is called "the spaghetti" because it is such a mess with roads and bypasses one on top of another. If you miss an exit because of the crazy way it twists around, you may have to drive what seems like 50 miles to recoup from your mistake. The trail out of Pieper Junction is close to the same as it twists back and forth like a loose noodle. Whatever the trail designers figured at that point is way beyond my imagination. Personally I think it's a stupid design, but it does give you plenty of opportunities to see if anybody is close behind you as it weaves back and forth way too many times, in my opinion. I actually prefer a trail that does not do that, because I don't like to have a rider behind me able to see me; it gives their horse a strong incentive to keep up, which, of course, is the nature of the beast.

I recall very well the 1978 Tevis, riding Eden's Cailana. I was in first place well ahead of the other riders when Kathie Perry and Marge Pryor caught up to me after crossing Highway 49. We were heading to Pointed Rocks, a half-hour vet check located near Cool, California and the last vet check before the finish line at Robie Point. Along that trail is a memorial to Paige Harper that Dru Barner (the first woman to win Tevis) and I created and installed right after Paige passed away. The climb past that memorial is steep and Kathie's horse, Prince Koslaif, stopped and would not continue. At that point, as I mentioned earlier. Kathie, who had an 8-minute advantage on me, was left behind. So as I entered the last vet check, I was once again in the lead all alone. All I had to do was get 9 minutes ahead of her and I would be the winner. Marge Pryor, riding Fritz, a one-eyed horse (who stayed with Kathie at that point) had started in a group #4. So Kathie and I, having started in groups 11 and 15, were way ahead of her as far as riding time went.

I am sure that confusion caused by group starts is the reason it was not always clear who the actual Tevis winner was at Robie Point until the next morning after Dru Barner and her bunch did all the calculations of the starting groups to see who actually won. Personally, that year I had the group numbers of the three riders that I was concerned about on a list inside my helmet. Marge Pryor was not on my list nor was Elwin Wines, a rider I passed in the canyon just before Devil's Thumb. So in essence, because Marge stayed with Kathie, her horse's companionship helped Prince Koslaif finally move on, so I didn't gain much time on Kathie. But I did gain a few minutes, which was critical at that point. Anyway, that's the reason I don't like the riders behind me to see me, but I like to see them if I can. So the "spaghetti trail" out of Pieper Junction will never be one of my favorite trails.

Anyway, back to the 2015 Pieper Junction vet check. All went well and one of the vets suggested I take a few extra minutes as Filouette looked a bit tired. YOU THINK! Those canyons were taxing on every horse, and we were still in the heat of the day. So I did take a few extra minutes and let my girl munch a bit of hay. This is a horse who seems to never get enough to eat, yet she was certainly not skinny.

When I left Pieper Junction I don't recall seeing any other riders arriving, so I was pretty confident I still had a good lead. But I knew there were still lots of riders on my tail — especially those with small numbers on their horses and #178. The trip down the next canyon is not that far to Foresthill, but it's a tough trip to the one-hour vet check, which is always a welcome stop.

POLE #8

FINALLY FORESTHILL!

THERE IS A paved road (Bath Road) the last stretch into Foresthill and it always seems like it's 15 miles long. It is uphill all the way, but thank goodness there is room on the side to avoid the pavement. Filouette was anxious to get there and set a nice steady trot all the way up. At this point ride spectators line the road, and there were a few at the beginning of the pavement, which is actually only about a mile — but a long mile. As we approached the top of the hill I could see hundreds of people cheering us on as I was the first rider in. Lots of happy spectators were delighted to assist with drinking water for my mare, as well as a garden hose to spray and cool down my hot and sweaty horse. I was a bit anxious to get checked in, but at the same time the crowd was so nice that it's good to slow down and take a few extra minutes to get through the area.

Vetting into Foresthill in first place is always a great feeling — one I have also experienced in the past. Again, the first rider into a vet check gets scrutinized very closely — all the vets were idle up to this point and they are happy to have something to do. Fact is that the first horse in is also a horse that has been ridden the fastest up to this point, so the possibility that that horse has been overridden is certainly a consideration. The downside is the veterinarians are definitely a bit more critical — perhaps extra points are made in front of the crowd of vets if one of them sees something wrong before the others do. It's hard to say, and in my opinion there is always room for error, especially if your horse steps on a rock or stumbles a bit during the trot out. I do think, however, that the vets all want the best for the horse and that is their first priority.

I recall in 2002 when I was first in at Foresthill riding Fayette De Cameo, and once again well ahead of the second rider. She was really off at the vet check trot out and I was happy to find a large rock wedged in her foot (a souvenir I still have on display at home). When the rock was removed she was fine and I ended up winning by over an hour that year. Fayette is the first and only Shagya Arabian to win the Tevis Cup as well as the Haggin Cup the year before in 2001.

The trot out at Foresthill has what seems like a few thousand spectators watching. You can bet that a few crews for other riders who are hoping their rider wins are also hoping your horse is lame. However, the vast majority of the people watching are wishing you well because they know what a difficult challenge it is just getting this far. As it turned out, this year I was asked to return before I left for a second look at Filouette. Nothing specific, as is the normal response from the vets, but just a second look.

So during this vet check I had one hour to relax a bit and let my famished horse eat some more, heaven forbid she starve to death. I had the assistance of a great crew — Kenny Mindt, a longtime friend, as well as a couple gals we always refer to as Bonnies Girls — Jordan Colleen Evans-Kirkpatrick and Tracy Martin. The 1977 Haggin Cup winner and a great friend from the past, Bill Fox, appeared out of nowhere after over 25 years of absence and he was a great help. Another rider, Andy Marlen, and two riders who were pulled early on — Gabriella Valsecchi and Michele Petty — were also there to cheer me on and do their best to assist in any way they could.

The Foresthill one-hour stop is always crowded with lots going on as riders pour in at a fast rate. It can be pretty hectic, so most riders seek a quiet place to take care of their horses. And since it is such a popular stop, it's very difficult to find solitude. It's nice to be close to the vetting area yet not so close that you don't have peace and quiet.

I sat in a chair while my crew kept pretty busy fussing over the horses. There is a lot of excitement everywhere and it is hard to just let the horse eat and relax — which I think is the best thing to do at this time. A rub down and fussing with the horse is not really necessary; I prefer to just let it be. As it turned out, sitting and resting was truly needed as my injury from the tumble down the hill on the Pucker Point trail had taken its toll. When I stood up the adrenalin had worn off from the fun of riding alone, and the pain set in from the fall. I could hardly walk back to do the recheck with the vets. Filouette was fine and we were given the go-ahead to continue.

I left the Foresthill vet check once again well ahead

of the other riders. Filouette was not happy leaving and I had to urge her on through town. Once we crossed Mosquito Ridge Road she was all business and we rode alone the entire way to just before Francisco's.

POLE #9

JUGGLING APPLES AT CAL 2; SOLITUDE (ALMOST) TO FRANCISCO'S

ONE STOP ALONG the way, from Foresthill to Francisco's Cal 2, was a nice treat with Lori Stewart and a few others there with water troughs for the horses. Lori told me I was quite a bit ahead of the other riders, which was good news as I knew there were plenty back there somewhere, but I had not heard or seen anyone behind me since leaving Foresthill. Lori insisted I take a couple of apples which she stuffed down the front of my shirt. She laughed as she said, "Now you know what us girls have to put up with!" as the apples juggled around on my chest. Later on I was happy to have those apples, as they are great thirst quenchers.

Filouette and I continued on, enjoying the views and the solitude of riding alone. That solitude was broken just a short distance from Francisco's when rider #178 flew past me at a gallop, followed by several more. I was shocked as I had not heard them approaching because they were going so fast. Filouette did not react much but she did offer to keep up with them, which was her normal reaction. But after a few cantering strides she was also happy to go back to a nice steady trot, which was our pace all day long except for those few times when the anxious riders galloped past us. So now I had slipped from 1st place to 4th or 5th as I recall. They moved so fast I don't remember how many passed me. Before long we approached a short upgrade into Francisco's vet check where there were a few water troughs — which was a nice surprise and a chance for those riders who passed me at a gallop to let their horses get a badly needed drink. Filouette didn't need any water because she tanked up at Cal 2, so once again, as I did at the turn off to the Pucker Point trail, I rode on past them. They were not too happy about that, so halfway to the vet-in point at Francisco's they came screaming past me. At that point Filouette asked me if she could smack'em back. I thought to myself, yes! — we deserve to be in first to the vet-in, so I let Filouette go and indeed we passed them all before we reached the top of the grade. A photo on FaceBook (posted by Elizabeth Speth) of me dismounting at that checkpoint shows #178's nose just behind me. She was the first of the three or four to pass me on the grade where we zipped past all of them just before the check-in. (See fig. 4)

Francisco's is a gate-and-go vet check and the volunteers there are anxious to help everyone. All the stops on the ride, the vet checks as well as the aid stops where volunteers are assisting everyone, are really great. In all the years I have been around Tevis, I have never experienced one person who didn't bend over backwards to help. My normal procedure at all vet checks, whether they are mandatory holds or a "gate-and-go," is the same. I immediately take the saddle off my horse, which helps them relax a bit as well as cool them down. Because time is important, I can remove and replace my

Fig 4: The nose of Rider #178's horse (last year's winning horse) was right behind me. Photo: The Arrival at Francisco's

saddle in less than one minute. That's why I always do it myself; if others do it differently it sometimes makes re-saddling a problem.   When I entered Francisco's, as usual I went straight to the water tubs. A volunteer immediately took Filouette's pulse. It was 64 so rather than unsaddle I took her to the vets. When the vet checked her pulse it was 72 so it was back to square one. I went back to the water tub and took her saddle off. As I glanced at the other riders, all of a sudden every one of them was doing the same. Saddles were flying everywhere. It made me laugh. As usual, Filouette's pulse dropped like a rock so I went right back to the vets and her pulse was down. We trotted out and got the go-ahead. As I exited the vet check area, someone asked if I needed anything. I responded, "Just my saddle" and bingo it was there. Less than a minute later I swung into the saddle and glanced across the area. Not one horse was heading to the vets yet, and none of them were saddled. As I rode out I thought to myself, "Ah ha! Once again there is no one in front of me."

I really enjoyed the next section. It overlooks one of my favorite spots on the American River where I often go swimming alongside a beautiful sandy beach I named "Studley Beach" long ago. It's a short drive from my ranch, and on the hottest days of summer there is hardly more than a half dozen people along that quarter mile of beach.

It wasn't long before I approached two guys riding a quad, hanging up glow sticks to mark the trail. They were a bit taken back when I called out to them over the roar of their vehicle. I think I spooked them a bit. I was still enjoying the pleasure of the daylight and solitude of the ride as I approached the group that assists the riders across the American River at Poverty Bar. Normally I stop and have a couple of bottles of beer with this bunch. I recall that the last time had beers with this group, they offered me one for the trail and I asked for one in a can. They gave me a can of Bud and I said, "That's not beer" and turned it down. They came up with a can of Coors, which is not much better as I prefer Corona. I said, "Don't open it; I'll do that after I cross the river." The reason I wanted a can instead of a bottle is I can crush the can and carry it to the next stop a lot easier than a bottle. It was dark that particular year and I broke the pull tab on that can, which gave me a real challenge. However, because I hardly ever go anywhere without my trusty Laguiole French knife, in addition to the blade it has a corkscrew as well as an awl. So I had a solution. Since it was dark I slowed to a walk and proceeded to poke a hole in the tab with the awl, and when I did the beer started spewing out and I nearly lost it all. My mount was a bit startled, but I managed to have what was left and continued on. Oh, the challenges we have on these rides.

POLE #10

CROSSING THE RIVER AND A RIGHT TURN TOWARD LOWER QUARRY

PFig 6: hoto: Eric Peach

A NYWAY, AS I approached the river crossing it was obvious the group of volunteers was surprised how early I was. The normal guidance system they have, which is a string of glow sticks on plastic bottles, was not installed yet. They offered me the usual beer, and I said, "No thanks, I'm in a bit of a hurry today." I didn't want to tell them I quit drinking alcohol long ago. So I entered the water and was shocked to see #178 upstream a ways from me. I had a big advantage because I knew the way, and where I was crossing was a lot shallower and she would probably have to swim. So I exited the water on the trail, but rider #178 was quick to catch up as we climbed out towards Maine Bar and the next vet check called Lower Quarry, on a single track trail. At this point the trail to my Sliger Mine Ranch cuts off to the left and my horses know that's the way home. However, they also know when we are riding Tevis we go to the right.

In 2004 a rider from back East, who had finished two years before riding my horse Cameo Corrine, crossed the river and because he was so fatigued and Cameo knew the way home, she turned left towards Sliger Mine Ranch and the tried rider let her. He had plenty of time to finish and we were all very concerned when he didn't show up. About 5:30 a.m. I got a call from a neighbor informing me Cameo had brought her rider home. Needless to say, he did not earn his third buckle.

However, this year rider #178 was on a horse that won this ride the year before, and that horse did not know about Sliger Mine Ranch so it didn't have that desire to go left. Of course they were right behind me as we scooted up the single track trail towards the next vet stop. It was not long before she asked to pass and I responded, "As soon as we get to the wider spot just ahead." When we did, I said, "I'll slow down and pull to the left (which was the downhill side) and let you by." She galloped by and disappeared quickly. I thought, oh well, second place is the first loser and that's not too bad. Now, as usual, Filouette was in the frame of mind to canter and stay with #178, but she is easy to control and agreed to just keep at a nice steady trot. From that point on it is about three miles to the next vet check Lower Quarry. So once again, Filouette and I were riding alone. It was so nice that she knows this trail very well and was happy.

When we reached the Lower Quarry vet stop, there was #178 trotting out her horse. I was surprised at the speed she was going — I expected her to be long gone. I entered the area immediately, unsaddled Filouette and gave her a drink and she was ready to go to the vets. The gang at that stop is always so nice and helpful with everything. All I needed was a couple glasses of that wonderful lemonade, which my great neighbor and top ten Tevis rider Judy Carnazzo offered with one in each hand, and to cool my horse down. As # 178 was leading back from the vets, I proceeded to the exam area and passed quickly. So back to my saddle and up-up-and-away I went. I was taken back a little when I noticed #178 still had not saddled up — but I was happy about that.

POLE #11

AN AUDIENCE
AT THE WORLD-FAMOUS
NO HANDS BRIDGE

THE TRAIL FROM Lower Quarry to the Highway 49 crossing is about two miles. It's a wide gravel road and there is a fair amount of traffic, but since it was just getting dark it was easy to avoid the traffic as well as pedestrians on the road. We crossed Highway 49 and climbed up the other side. It was pretty dark now, but the trail was marked very well with glow sticks, and of course we both knew practically every inch of it down to No Hands Bridge. There was a big crowd at No Hands that cheered me on, and of course offered help if needed. Andy Marlen was there with a bottle of Replenish (which is a healthy replacement for Gatorade which I consider junk) that Gabriella had prepared for me but I didn't really need anything. So it was on across No Hands, where there was quite a crowd on the actual bridge as well as on both ends.

That moment reminded me of the time many years ago on a training ride with Paige Harper and Diane Hall when we galloped across that bridge before the railings were installed. Diane said, "Wow, that was the first time I ever galloped across this bridge let alone three abreast!" Paige replied, "Hah! And I will never do it again!" Anyway, it was pretty dark now and the moon had not blessed us with the magic glow of the sun so it was pretty hard to see the trail. Knowing Filouette could see much better than I could, we continued on at a nice trot.

I have never, and probably never will do, that glow stick stuff where riders attach glow sticks in every place imaginable on their horse as well as carry a flashlight of some sort either on their helmet or in their saddle pack. However, I do recall just once I was happy the rider in front of me had a light. That was in 2009, riding out of Francisco's with Mr. Seiichi Hasumi, when we were in 10th and 11th place. It was 10:30 p.m. and it was dark and too early for moonshine. The trail out is a twisty, rocky, downhill, narrow path with lots of trees. It was pitch black. Mr. Hasumi had a light on his helmet that was very bright and it lit up the whole trail like it was daylight. He was riding SMR Fayette de Cameo, the horse I won the Tevis Cup on in 2002, and I was on Filouette. I was suffering from a bad kick on my left knee sustained a few months earlier and it was a bit sore. When we got to the road that leads up to the cutoff to the river crossing, Mr. Hasumi and Fayette set a great pace and I was not prepared to ride that fast with my knee injury. I will never forget the incredible trot that Fayette had so I knew Mr. Hasumi was going to do well.

One other time I recall when a light was handy was in 1993 when Michel Bloch, Renaud Nuel and I rode together; it was the first time those two Frenchmen rode Tevis and it was quite a day. We left the Lower Quarry vet check about 2 a.m. and as we approached the trail above Highway 49 leading to No Hands Bridge, it was very dark in that heavily wooded section of the trail. The horses all stopped and would not go forward. Finally Renaud pulled out a flashlight (I didn't even know he had one) and we could see the trail made a very sharp right turn. Those days glow sticks were pretty expensive and were sparsely spaced on the trail. So there have been exceptions to having a light. In both of these cases I am sure it would not have been a disaster without the lights, but they sure made it a bit better.

So as Filouette and I continued down the trail this year, the moon finally appeared which made travel a bit more comfortable. Finally we saw a cluster of lights set up by volunteer Robert Sydnor that were strung across the new bridge that bypassed a drop down to a stream that provided a nice cool drink of water. Mr. Sydnor was very clear with directions on both routes — over the bridge or around it where a drink of water was a possibility. Filouette and I selected the old original path down to the stream and I could hear her drinking so it was a good decision. I counted about eight or nine sips of water and she was ready to go again.

POLE #12

FINISH LINE IN VIEW —
AND
A 4000 MILE BUCKLE IN SIGHT

OUR NEXT SIGN of life was at Robie Point where a handful of people, happy to see us, cheered the riders on. It brought back memories when that was the finish line and it would be pretty crowded. Those days we officially finished at Robie Point, yet we had to walk up Robie Drive past the homes of Hal Hall, Dru Barner, Jack Veal and a few other notables, then ride on through residential streets up to the railroad tracks and follow them down to Pacific Avenue and across to the fairgrounds.   There was no such thing as glow sticks, and splats of white chalk on the road were the guidance system. Once in a while a rider would get lost in the residential area but not for long.

So from Robie Point to the finish line we rode along at a nice easy trot and up to the current finish. There was a huge crowd — the largest I have ever seen waiting to see us — and it was a super feeling to hear the loud cheers and clapping. I gave Filouette a drink and Tom Johnson, a notable accomplished rider and runner, was there to assist me on into the fairgrounds for my victory lap and final vet check. It was a nice walk and I was glad he was there, as I didn't know they had changed the route from the finish line to the Gold Country Fair-

Fig 6: The bandage is still on my arm from the fall down the hill on Pucker Point Trail
Photo Credit: Bill Gore

grounds. I can't imagine why the change was made from the preliminary vet check right there near the actual finish, which is close to a nice place to vet. They have done that for years to prevent someone who finished on an obviously lame horse entering the fairgrounds and trotting around the arena in front of the crowd. That would have been a big negative image for the event. Interesting change in presentation for sure.

When you get to the gate into the stadium it's time to present yourself to the waiting crowd. That's where Tom Johnson left me. I mounted Filouette and we trotted around the arena to the official finish line under the Tevis finish banner. *(See fig. 6)*

We were then introduced by Pete Occhialini, who has a write-up on all the riders. Pete has been doing this role now for quite a few years and does an outstanding job. Pete has a challenge in his position as announcer because sometimes the horses come in single or in groups. When they come in groups, Pete's talent is taxed but he still does a remarkable job. So after coming under the banner, I dismounted and we had a brief chat for the benefit of the spectators, and I was overwhelmed by the greetings of the crowd. I couldn't believe the number of cheerful and smiling children who wanted a photo with me and it was very nice to see all the smiles and hear all the salutations.

Meanwhile, my efficient crew was busy taking care of Filouette and preparing her to be presented to the vets for her final examination. That examination takes place right there in the arena and the crowd watches closely for the vets to indicate their approval, when your finish is assured and you have earned your Tevis buckle.

In the 40-plus years I have been around Tevis, the year 2013 was without a question one of my most memorable at the final vet check. That is the year Ragan Kelly rode SMR Fifi d'Or (my homebred mare who won the Tevis Cup in 2005 *) along with her mother, Tracy Kelly DVM, from Waco, Texas. A Tevis buckle had been on Tracy's bucket list for 20 years and she never imagined that one day her 12-year-old daughter would say, "Mom, I want to ride Tevis too." So when Ragan and I presented Fifi d'Or to the vets for her final exam and Dr. Fellers handed her vetting slip back with a big smile and congratulated her, I had goosebumps big time. What a wonderful feeling to know I helped that lovely young rider and her mother get a buckle. Incidentally, Ragan received one of the Legacy Buckles donated by Julie Suhr, who has finished Tevis 22 times. Julie's daughter, Barbara White, has finished the ride 34 times and currently holds the record for most buckles earned. It was very heartwarming when Julie and Ragan were photographed together at the awards banquet.

The Legacy Buckle program was instituted a few years back when riders who had lots of buckles donated them to the ride to present free of charge to riders who earned their first buckle. I expect that Legacy program to be available again in the future when more buckles are donated back to new riders. There are three riders who each sport one of my buckles from years gone by: Lene Hammeren from Norway finished in 6th place on SMR Filouette in 2014, Willimina DeBoar from the Netherlands finished 7th in 2012 on SMR Filouette, and

Robert Weldin earned one in 2011. After all, you really only need two buckles, one for general wear and a nice shiny one for dress.

Speaking of shiny buckles — when Wendell Robie earned his 1000 mile buckle in 1968 he ordered it in gold. The 1000 miles buckle is awarded to riders who complete the ride ten times. A 20-time completion qualifies you for the 2000 mile buckle, and completing 30 times earns you the 3000 mile buckle. I am counting on earning the 4000 mile buckle perhaps I will be age 90 but that is just a number. So my 4000 mile buckle should be in Gold as well, why not?

I told Wendell that when I got my 1000 mile buckle I wanted mine in gold too. His response was, "Well, Potato, start saving your money now so you can pay for it." So in 2009 when I earned my 2000 mile buckle, I got it in gold. So that's my shiny buckle. Of course, it's pretty hard to give away one of the winning Tevis buckles because they're unique. Each winners buckle is inscribed with the year of winning as well as on the top banner is the word "winner." In spite of the AERC slogan, "To finish is to win," there is only one winning Tevis buckle. In that same frame of reference, some say it should just be called a "ride," but if it's not a race why give a winner's buckle, why have top ten awards and why do so many riders want to finish first?

Back to 2015. We presented and passed the final vetting without a problem. Filouette was ready to continue for sure. The next rider, #4, arrived 30 minutes later. I was very happy to see Dawn Tebbs, #54, one of my frequent riding companions who also keeps her horse at

Sliger Mine Ranch, arrive in 6th place just over an hour later. This was Dawn's first top ten finish and her second buckle. Last year she finished 41st,, her first time riding Tevis, on an Arab/Friesian cross mare bred by Patricia Chappell who has earned 20 Tevis buckles — 13 of them riding a Quarter Horse mare named Thunders Lightning Bar, who was 20-years-old on her last finish. That's a record for the Quarter Horse breed. Dawn and her husband Dan own a bicycle shop in Auburn, and both are champions in the bicycle sport world. Dawn's first entry into the endurance world was in 2013 when she rode a few rides. Then she really got serious in 2014 when she moved her horse to my Sliger Mine Ranch. So in 2014 Dawn finished in 41st place on the same horse she rode this year to 6th place, so it was a nice improvement for her.

Now here's another "Potato Rule." You're not allowed to leave the fairgrounds if you finish in top ten until after Haggin Cup judging takes place at 10 a.m. Sunday morning. That rule came about in 1998 when I won the Tevis Cup riding SMR Fille de Cailana. After the finish I asked and received permission from the vets to take Fille home where she could spend the night in her own 35-acre pasture. I brought her back in the morning in time for the Haggin Cup judging and someone made a stink about me doing that.

Normally I have more than one horse in the event, so I have to wait for everyone to finish anyway, so I generally take my horse — or horses as the case may be — to my trailer in the back upper field where it is a lot quieter and everyone can rest. When all my riders are finished

I take them to home to Sliger Mine Ranch.   This year there was a box stall provided for the first ten horses to finish. That was nice for Filouette, and I'm sure she felt special about that. I felt pretty good, so I stayed around a while to watch other riders come in. Finally one of the great bunch helping me all day (Andy Marlen) insisted I get some rest in his trailer that was well equipped.

A few hours sleep was nice and then I drove home to prepare for the Sunday morning festivities. The Native Sons of the Golden West always have a food concession at the fairgrounds where they serve a great breakfast with all the fixings. It's also a great place to socialize with friends and check out the final results of the ride. The last riders usually come in pretty close to the 24-hour cut-off time at 5:15 a.m. So there is plenty of activity all night long and the volunteers, as well as the vets, are taxed to the limit energy-wise by that time.

POLE #13

Presenting at Haggin Cup Judging; Eating Oats at Awards Ceremony

I T WAS A very nice sunny Sunday morning and the accolades for my win were overwhelming. I truly never expected such a reaction. And I never thought of myself as old until I saw a headline of a 73-year-old winning the Tevis. Actually, I was only 72 but I never gave much thought to my age — age is just a number. Now I have to remember I'm old, but not too old to ride a horse or work out at the gym three or four times a week. As a matter of fact, I don't consider myself too old to do much of anything.

So I had no problem taking my mare to the Haggin Cup judging and trotting her out. The Haggin Cup (best condition) award, by the way, is considered by many to be the most coveted award because it is supposedly based on the horse who did the best job over all. That, of course, is a matter of judgment because of the variables involved as well as the input being subjective. But there's no question that it's a much-respected award. However, I do wish I had run a bit slower when I was told to trot Filouette out about 150 feet and back, then in a circle both directions. It's a large circle, giving the vets as well as the audience in the bleachers plenty of time to see just how "fit to go on" each horse is.

There is a video available on the internet of me trotting Filouette out. I like what I see so much, that next time I will run slower so the video is longer! In my eyes she looked wonderful. The first ten riders to finish are given the opportunity to present their horse for inspection at the Haggin Cup judging if they want, where the horses are assessed for being in the best condition to go on. Normally all top ten horse and rider teams are present for that occasion. The fact is that the top finishers quite often look a lot better than the rest of the finishers the next day. That's because of many reasons; one is they are usually in great shape. Of course there are many other aspects to consider. The judging takes into consideration several factors, and the only one that is really subjective is the horse's condition.

In other AERC rides, the rider's weight and number of minutes behind the winning time are taken into consideration for best condition awards, so a heavyweight rider finishing beside a lightweight rider has a distinctive advantage. However, the Tevis does not adhere to that AERC rule.

In February 2015 I lost the Best Condition award on another ride by two points to a heavyweight rider who finished in third place on a 100-mile race that I won on Filouette. He finished well over an hour behind me. Because it's a subjective judgment, the fact that many vets take part in the procedure gives it credibility. Actually, the real procedure is top secret with the examining committee so it is hard to say what really goes on with that bunch.

After the Haggin Cup judging at Tevis, the person who I had trailered to the ride with wanted to take her horse back to the ranch, so soon after the judging we took our horses back to Sliger Mine Ranch.

The awards banquet and presentation of the finishing awards is always a grand affair at the fairgrounds. It's lots of fun and time to socialize with other riders and, of course, see the Top Ten winning horses and find out who won the Haggin Cup. Halfway through the awards presentation I remembered that top ten riders were to present our mounts one at a time to receive our awards, which is generally a cooling blanket, ribbon for the horse, and of course the buckle. And the actual winner also receives a round gold pendant. This presentation of all top ten horses had completely escaped my mind — probably due to all the excitement I was receiving over being such an old person to win the ride. Another factor is I had not finished in top ten since 2006 when I placed 3rd riding my Shagya stallion SMR Garcon. That year we had the awards banquet across the way in the fairgrounds in a nice amphitheater setting that was a lot more accommodating and the presentation of top ten was much easier.

This year I had taken Filouette home and therefore could not possibly present her at the awards ceremony. I was very disappointed and it was too late to go home and get her. So rather than the usual procedure of letting the winning horse eat a bit of grain out of the top of the beautiful perpetual Tevis Cup sterling trophy, I took a handful of grain myself and ate it for the crowd. The next 48 hours were absolutely incredible as one person after another contacted me to express their congratulations. Many told me their age and said, "By golly, if you can do that at your age, it gives me hope too." The day after the ride was over and I was back at Sliger Mine Ranch, I was astonished at the amount of feedback on the ride that was available on the internet.

Quite frankly, the whole episode gave me a new perspective on my age; now I think of myself as a lot older. As a matter of fact, several years ago I ran in a marathon and when I inspected the results, I noticed that the fastest runner in the five-year-age groups was always slower than the slowest runner in the next higher age group. So age does make a difference. It also makes me think about next year in a different light. I certainly plan to ride Tevis again in 2016 and furthermore, as I mentioned earlier, the 4000 mile buckle is a good goal, WHY NOT?

So here I am after over 40 years of being involved with this incredible event. Looking back over the years, I am very happy that my three children are all Tevis buckle earners. My son Range has three buckles from the years 1997, 1998 and 2000. My daughter Tricia earned her buckle as a junior rider in 1983 when we rode the Frontier Division together, which meant no crew was allowed. It was so much fun. I will never forget when we crossed No Hands Bridge only a few miles from the finish line at Robie Point. I asked her how she was doing and she replied, "Dad, this is so much fun!" After winning Tevis this year, Tricia told me her 14-year-old daughter Taylor now wants to ride Tevis too. Now I have another goal — to see Taylor earn a Tevis buckle and perhaps my grandson Jordan too, who is a couple years younger. It will, indeed, be my pleasure. My other daughter Denise rode the ride in 1979 on a horse named Ferraz that I got from Paige Harper's widow Genevieve. Denise finished 33rd out of a starting group of 227.

I cannot begin to list all the riders from many other countries that I have had the great pleasure of assisting in earning their Tevis buckle. I can, however, list the countries: Africa, England, Germany, Norway, Netherlands, France, Hungary, Brazil, Italy, Wales, Spain and the UAE. And I'm not done yet. Now Portugal is on the list for 2016. In addition, there have been many riders from all over the United States who I have had the pleasure of helping cross the finish line.

POLE #14

WHAT LED TO MY SUCCESS?

I ONCE HEARD JIM Rohn, the world famous American entrepreneur, author and motivational speaker, whom I greatly admire, say, "Everything matters." This quote most often comes to mind when I'm at the gym, pushing myself to go one more rep, or perhaps cutting my workout short because of time constraints.

Of course Paige Harper, Wendell Robie and Dru Barner — as I mentioned earlier — had significant influences on my riding. One of my fondest recollections of Paige was early on as we rode along a trail on Folsom Lake. As we talked, I told Paige how Grazeagle Bandit (my first endurance horse) nearly slipped on a switchback with a steep drop-off. Paige told me how important it is to have complete faith in your horse. That memory has served me well over the years. I recall once on the John Muir Trail that I was certain death was on my doorstep, but my confidence in Cailana was critical, and she performed an incredible maneuver that most likely saved my life. This year on Tevis on the Pucker Point trail, as I was sliding down the rocky edge of the steep hill, Filouette was smarter than me and refused to climb up that steep bank with me on her back. That particular challenge made Cougar Rock look like child's play.

Filouette was also smart enough to not follow me

down the same way I slid down in order to land on the trail. So having confidence in your horse is a critical lesson.

For over 20 years I've used the horse products of Dynamite Specialty Products. There are several products that I always have on hand. First, Dynamite+ is a multi-vitamin grain specially formulated for the soil where I live. Next is a free choice minerals selection of four products that cover 98% of the minerals horses need and don't always get from their hay or grain. That selection consists of all natural salt and three other mineral combinations. I keep their dispensers stocked all the time so the minerals are readily available.

Next is the Pelleted Grain Ration (PGR), a high quality grain ration that is chemical free (I think they call that organic) consisting of oats, corn and barley plus a few other things including the Dynamite+ mentioned above. My favorite Dynamite product is Pre-Race Pak. Because of this feeding routine, I have never worried about electrolytes. I feed Pre-Race the three days before the ride, twice a day (morning and night) and at least two hours before the start of the ride as well as during the ride. I have an old-fashioned meat grinder that I use to grind up lots of carrots to mix the Pre-Race, PGR and other goodies in, so the horses love it. Depending on the horse, I may add a bit more of some of the free choice minerals. I have learned from some great medical professionals a technique called kinesiology and use it daily, especially with my horses. One of my mares seemed to be tripping a bit now and then. With the kinesiology technique, I discovered that a little extra of the Dynamite 1 to 1 mix in her grain eliminated that problem.

I am always amazed when I see so many riders with syringes of electrolytes and additional who-knows-what sticking out of their saddle packs. As a matter of fact, just as I was approaching Cougar Rock something fell out of the saddle packs of the rider in front of me. It happened so fast I didn't see what is was. I called out to the rider that she lost something and a rider behind me said it was vet wrap. For the life of me, I can't imagine why someone would carry vet wrap on the ride. I don't even carry a water bottle — just my trusty Laquoile French knife.

Another product that I am very happy with is what I call "Ted's Stuff" or just TS for short. It is a bio-Nano-technology cleaner that is actually just that — a cleaner. Because of the "Nano" term it is so powerful that it destroys (what I've been told) all the bacteria, germs and even the viruses that inhibit healing of wounds and other injuries. As a matter of fact, SMR Fifi d'Or years ago would come back from a trail ride and sometimes be covered with lots of ticks. I can't explain why, but I bathed her in TS and never again did she have anywhere near the number of ticks on her. The TS is very versatile; I even use it as a plant spray in my garden and also on any rashes or cuts on my body. It is also a great laundry soap and liquid dish soap. I also have it in a hand dispenser by my sink.

Speaking of bathing, my water system is absolutely the best. For over 20 years I have had a device on my water line that revitalizes the water into what I refer to as "Living Water." The benefits of this water are beyond belief. If you Google "Grander Revitalized Water" you will find lots of information. I even have a portable unit I take sometimes when I travel, such as when I went to Abu Dhabi with Fayette de Cameo.

I normally take a supply of this Living Water with me on rides, and when I run out my horses let me know right away. It was amusing to see one of my young horses at the Pieper Junction (Chicken Hawk) vet stop on Tevis going from water trough to water trough looking for good water. She finally looked around and sort of gave me a sigh and drank what she could find. I could tell you lots of great examples of the value of this water, and I believe it's one more reason I don't need to carry water with me on rides. The revitalized water, in my opinion, is a miracle in the way it works. I firmly believe that if everybody in the world used this type of water it would have a major impact on our environment and health. I have shared this device all over the world and will continue to do so.

Riders who keep their horses barefoot are not going to be very happy about this. But I am determined to keep things simple, and the few times I have, for whatever reason, used rubber boots or even pads I have not been successful. Many riders use rubber boots with consistent success and I'm sure it's because they get a lot of practice putting them on. I recall a ride earlier this year (2015) when a rider was sticking to me like glue to the first vet check. Just before we arrived at the checkpoint I noticed a red mark on the side of his horse's hoof. Turns out it was the remaining piece of a red rubber boot. I don't recall seeing him again on the trail after the vet check but he did finish.   I lost that 50-mile ride, incidentally, by half a neck length. If you insist on using rubber boots like EasyBoots, I suggest you go to the EasyCare (Tevis official sponsor) website or watch a demonstration. They are experts and will be happy to show you all the options.

My opinion is the same about pads. I used pads twice on Tevis many years ago and each time I lost a shoe. The two times I used pads was at the insistence of the owner of the horse I rode.   Many years ago when I first started riding a lot of rides in Europe, quite a few manufacturers of plastic shoes gave me samples to try and not a single one of them worked for me. So all these years I still use iron shoes. The technology of equine feed and products is always changing, and it's impossible to keep up with it — so I don't even try. I just enjoy what works for me and that includes iron horseshoes.

I did get talked into trying special boots once. I was mentored by a barefoot specialist. The whole argument made sense to me because I was taking my mare SMR Fayette de Cameo to a 160 km race in Abu Dhabi.   I figured the larger hoofprint in the Persian Gulf desert sand would be an advantage. Turns out, it seemed like the whole 100 miles was graded before the race so I stuck to the iron shoes. I will never forget the struggles I had getting used to those rubber boots. It's funny to look back at that experience.

When I got my first endurance horse while living at Paige Harper's ranch apartments, he fed all his horses straight alfalfa. He was my mentor, so I have done the same ever since. I still, to this day, hear the argument that alfalfa is too much protein or whatever. All I know is it works for me, so I firmly believe in that statement, "If it ain't broke, don't fix it."

Another factor that leads to my success is helping others enjoy the sport. I truly do enjoy helping others ride, and especially helping others ride Tevis. If — heaven forbid — I was never able to ride, I would still continue to do my best to introduce others to the Tevis 100 Mile One Day Ride. My great friend, Romano Macri, left this world due to heart failure of some sort five miles from the finish line of a 70 km ride in Italy. That's the way I would prefer to go, or perhaps right after the finish line would be better.

On one particular ride in 1994, Romano rode a horse named Zion, Thomas Juergens from Germany rode SMR Jeune Fille (the dam of SMR Fifi d'Or) and I rode SMR Fille de Cailana (my 1998 Tevis Cup winner). This was Romano's and Thomas' first United States ride, a 50-mile ride called Washoe Valley 50. We were all in the top ten with Fille in 2nd place, winning BC. That was Romano's only ride in America, but Thomas continued to acquire nearly 1000 miles riding with me all over the western United States, including Tevis, of course.

When thinking of helping others, one great memory I have is of Linda Gruver in 1994 riding the OutLaw Trail. The OutLaw Trail was a five-day, 265-mile ride put on by Crockett and Sharon Dumas in the 1990's — a fantastic event in beautiful southern Utah. If you finished all five days on the same horse, you were considered an outlaw. You could switch horses on each day or perhaps not ride every day or not finish each day. With any of those situations, you were considered a Pinkerton. The Pinkerton National Detective Agency was founded in Chicago in 1850. The Pinkertons were riders from the Old West hired by Wells Fargo to find the outlaw gang known as Butch Cassidy and the Sundance Kid bunch.

Each night around the Outlaw Trail endurance ride campfire, after the daily completion awards, the stories would begin. One particular Wednesday night, an old timer who grew up in the area we were riding told stories of "way back when." The ride the next day went through a canyon about 15 miles long. The sides of the canyon walls were hundreds of feet high and the trail just followed the river below. The old timer played his guitar and whistled as he sang songs that told of a great flood in years gone by. Those descriptions were so interesting as he described the sound of great walls of water rushing down the canyons — one of which was the very canyon we were to ride the next day. He spoke of many lost lives and buildings destroyed in the floods. You could hear a pin drop as he told of the disasters.

That very night a storm blew in and alarms were sounded, indicating that we may have to abandon camp immediately. There were probably 50 rigs in camp and all of the people were upset. As time passed, the evacuation order was dismissed, but the ride was possibly cancelled for that day. Finally, Butch (aka Crockett Dumas — many of the riders had outlaw nicknames) announced the ride that day was on, but no penalty would be assessed and a full refund would be given if a rider chose not to ride. Linda Gruver was a crew member for me and a riding companion named Julie Weaver who said in no uncertain terms would she ride. So I asked Linda if she wanted to do her very first endurance ride, and she was anxious to go. Julie told her she was crazy. But it turned out to be a great day and Julie turned into a Pinkerton rider along with Linda. Linda was hooked and a few years later rode many rides on those same trails, but never became an outlaw. Linda and I did finish that first ride of hers in top ten. She rode a horse named Zion who later became a Tevis finisher for the young man from France named Renaud Nuel. I rode Fille de Cailana that year, and every year I rode the Outlaw Trail rides I was an outlaw rider. Renaud rode Zion on Tevis in 1993 and was an Outlaw Trail rider with me in 1993 as well.

For all my life I have tried to keep things simple. When I started riding endurance many years ago, I did it for the fun and enjoyment of being on a horse. The day I don't enjoy that feeling, I will hang up my spurs (so to speak) and spend more time snow skiing or maybe scuba diving. I do enjoy a game of golf but I prefer the physically demanding activities a lot more.

So I have set my goals for 2016 and beyond. I can't imagine why I shouldn't be the oldest rider to earn a 4000 mile Tevis buckle. I just need to be consistent like Barbara White who has 34 buckles and Hal Hall who has 30.

See you down trail!

END NOTES:

LEARN FROMTHREE TIME WINNER
OF
THE TEVIS CUP AND STILL GOING

POTATO HAS FINISHED TEVIS 22 TIMES
OUT OF 31 STARTS 9 TIMES IN TOP TEN
LET HIM SHARE HIS EXPERIENCE WITH
YOU ON THE TRAILS AS WELL AS IN
COMPETITIONS

POTATO OFFERS TEVIS BOOTCAMPS
EXPERIENCE TEVIS TRAILS
LEARN TEVIS TRAILS
www.tevispost.com

28152602R00054

Made in the USA
Middletown, DE
05 January 2016